Stretching the Dollar:

Discover The Secrets Of Spending With Less

Legal & Disclaimer

The information contained in this book is not designed to replace or take the place of any form of medical or professional medical advice. The information in this book has been provided for educational and entertainment purposes only.

The information contained in this book has been compiled from sources deemed reliable, and it is accurate to the best of the Author's knowledge; however, the Author cannot guarantee its accuracy and validity and cannot be held liable for any errors or omissions. Changes are periodically made to this book. You must consult your doctor or get professional medical advice before using any of the suggested remedies, techniques, or information in this book.

Upon using the information contained in this book, you agree to hold harmless the Author from and against any damages, costs, and expenses, including any legal fees, potentially resulting from the application of any of the information provided in this guide. This disclaimer applies to any damages or injury caused by the use and application, whether directly or indirectly, of any advice or information presented, whether for breach of contract, tort, negligence, personal injury, criminal intent, or under any other cause of action.

You agree to accept all risks of using the information presented in this book. You need to consult a professional medical practitioner in order to ensure you are both able and healthy enough to participate in this program.

Contents

Introduction - Your Money Personality

Budgeting is big news these days, as families are feeling the squeeze. Money may have always been tight but it seems that the way things are going it's only getting tighter still. We all want to know how to stretch those pennies further. It's such a simple thing to do, so congratulate yourself on being ahead of the curve and learning this important skill.

There are 5 distinct personalities that people exhibit when it comes to money - spenders, savers, risk averse, gamblers, and fliers.

Spenders are those who rarely save a penny and seem to run through their money like water. They will spend their money first and think about the consequences later. Spenders are often personalities that are generous to their friends and supporters of many charitable causes. Savers, on the other hand, are fervent bargain hunters and are often hard to part with their money. Savers are often resourceful and can be viewed as cheapskates. These are the two personalities you'll recognize easily, and there's a good chance you're not much of a saver if you're trying to learn more about budgeting.

The risk-averse are those who use their money strategically and are all about planning. They invest money and see it as a tool for security. You can learn a lot from them as they are the ones planning a solid financial future. Gamblers are the opposite, they are all about the big payoff at the end and tend to use their money with instinct and luck. For those who are lucky they may have winning investments, but there's also a huge chance they could gamble and lose it all at any times.

The fliers are the happy-go-lucky people that don't really think about money. It exists, but it doesn't create status, or act like a tool, and they don't really mind if they have a lot or a little at the end of the day.

Most people are either one of these types outright or they lean towards two of them. Do you see yourself in any of these?

The key to learning successful budgeting techniques is knowing the type of spender personality that you are, and the type of spender that you want to be in order to save money. The most successful savers are those who are also somewhat risk-averse - they save their money, but wisely use some of it to plan a solid future. Even if you're a flier who likes to save, you can still be a success with budgeting.

So, think about how you see money and how you spend it. If you're not a saver or a risk-averse type yet, then this book can definitely help you get there.

Hopefully, you'll learn a few important tools along the way and get on the road to better financial independence through planning.

Once you're through with the book we'd love for you to leave us a great review.

Chapter 1 - Need vs Want

The first step when it comes to learning budgeting techniques is to know what sort of monetary amount you're working with. If you're only working with your own income then this is quite simple since you know what you're making. If you're working as a household with pooled resources find the number that is the sum of everything that everyone makes. Some people have paycheques that fluctuate week to week, don't worry, this isn't a budgeting issue just take the average amount over the month and use that number as your weekly pay cheques. Got it?

Let's say that your family makes about $2700 a month. It's not a whole lot, but you already know that. Think of this number as a bucket. Your $2700 bucket is full of water (money). You'll take a cup of water for each of your bills - rent, electric, etc. Once your bills have come out, there is still water left in that bucket for food, gas, and other expenses. The problem is that your bucket has a hole in it, and it's causing the water to run out. Even if you know you have enough water to cover the number of cups you need sometimes you're short. Budgeting aims to plug that hole up.

Addicted to Consuming

Most of us like having new things. They make us happy. The problem is that this happiness is empty and temporary. As consumers, we're addicted to the high we get from buying things we don't need because it gives us a boost, not only that it can also make us forget for that little moment that we have problems or bills waiting on us. Being happy is not a crime, but thinking that these items you're buying make you happy is not only a poor substitute but it's a recipe for getting into debt. We often buy things we don't need, even things that we don't need right now, but will need in the future or simply because it's a "good deal".

When you go to the grocery store for the week how much of that food ends up being wasted? Do you find yourself throwing away leftovers? The grocery store is one of the biggest holes in your financial bucket. We waste millions every year on food that just gets thrown away or food that we don't need. It's not just the grocery store, when we buy clothes we rarely think about the fact that we have 10 more of the same item at home, just not the same as the one in front of us. We don't need it.

Identifying Needs

The biggest obstacle to why you haven't been successful in budgeting, is that you've failed to identify the difference between want and need. A need is something that we have an immediate use for, it is an essential, something that our lives would be lacking without. That new shirt that you need for a job interview because you've outgrown the old one. That is a need. The ingredients to make dinner tonight. That is a need. The third pair of Jimmy Choos, which look rather similar to the other 10 pairs you own - that's not a need.

The opposite of needs is wanting. Wants are things that we don't necessarily need, but we want for whatever reason. Wants are items and things that we can do without, they may make our lives easier or we may have created an artificial feeling that our lives will be enriched by owning the item. A want is a new pair of black boots, maybe they're on sale or they're a little different, but you've also still got a perfectly good pair at home. They're not going to help you earn more money, they're not going to make you more financially stable, and you've already got something in that space in your closet. You don't need the boots, but you want them.

An exercise one of my friends did was to identify a financial goal and then whenever she spent her money she would ask herself if she wanted the item more than that financial goal. By doing this, she held herself accountable to purchasing based on her priorities and not just on wants and needs.

Prioritizing

Once you can start identifying the things you need over the things you want, you can start to prioritize your spending. Priorities are something we all have, we're all familiar with them. For some bills are a priority, they make sure that they are paid first before spending any other money. Others may see food and day to day expenses as more important or even those happy go lucky people that buy the new pair of shoes above everything because it makes them feel happy for that moment.

Think about all the things in your life. What is important to you? Is it the place you live? Is it keeping your children fed? What is your priority?

You may have 2 or 3 different priorities, you may have even more than that.

Exercise: Think back on that $2700 bucket. What would you spend each drop of water on each month? On a piece of paper, list your spending that money from 1 -10 with 1 being the most important. You can also list it as an equation with the total being $2700 if it makes it easier. An estimate of the amount you spend. Take a look at this list and identify whether or not these priorities are wants or needs. Would you be able to live without them?

Did you manage to cross anything off that list? You've already learned a new skill. What you just did was to identify whether you needed or wanted something that is in your monthly spending. This is just a start. Those priorities are still going to have ways within them to tighten your spending up.

Importance of Saving

Most people will not have listed saving money on that list. Fewer than 50% of people actively save money. It's suggested that you have at least 6 months worth of money to cover everyday bills put aside in case of emergency. But for those struggling week to week, this seems a dream. Once you've started budgeting your money properly you'll find you've got that little bit more room to save money that you never thought you had. Some people can get pretty extreme with this.

You've heard of the extreme couponers? They pinch every penny out of their grocery list and sometimes even manage to make their money back by only shopping using coupons. The reason saving money is so important is that it goes back to the 5 types of spenders. Those who are risk averse see money as stability

Think about the most successful people in the world. Do you think they are spenders or savers? Would you say that these people invest their money wisely or gamble it?

The one thing ALL financially successful people have in common is that they are risk-averse savers. They are successful not because they don't spend their money at all but because they spend it wisely so that it grows. They base their security on the fact that should anything happen they have money to fall back on. This is one of the main reasons that it is suggested for you to have at least 6 months of personal savings - just in case.

Now, think about your $2700 bucket. How much of that money could you put aside? $10? $100? You're probably thinking no way, you can barely make ends meet never mind saving money. Budgeting is how you're going to achieve that goal.

Chapter 2 - Give a Man a Fish

The truth is that saving isn't difficult, it's about being smarter with your money and making your money work for you. Those successful people often started in the same place as you, but they invested wisely and grew their money until they are where they are at today. If you've ever heard the saying about "give a man a fish" then you'll know that teaching to fish is the long term goal. What we're going to do now is teach you how to fish. You CAN save, no matter how small your budget is or how much money you make every week. It's all something that can be solved by having the right tools.

Myths of budgeting

MYTH: Budgeting Prevents You From Spending

Instead of looking at your budget as a way of limiting excess spending, start looking at it as a way of spending smarter. You're getting more of the things you want by simply reorganizing how you spend your money. Even if you're living paycheck to paycheck a budget is all about spending the money you have wiser, not avoiding spending it at all. It goes back to the concept of priorities. Your priority is bills and food, but if you're budgeting and sourcing those things correctly, you can still have a little wiggle room.

MYTH: Budgets are Strict

Budgeting is like dieting, too strict and you may get frustrated and quit, too flexible and you won't budget at all. A good budget is somewhere in the middle so that you can still enjoy your money while still keeping your priorities in mind. Life isn't always predictable, and sometimes you will stray outside your budget. It's just a fact. Stressing over that one time isn't helpful, and it's going to make you less inclined to keep budgeting because you'll see it as a negative thing. As long as you don't make a habit of going outside your budget it isn't a problem if you keep it flexible.

MYTH: You Must be Good at Maths to Budget

The days of sitting with a calculator and a pencil adding figures up are long gone. This is a poor excuse why you can't budget. In these days of convenience, there is even on the go app software so you can log purchases as you make them and balance your chequebook without having to ever open it. Many programs like this are free and safe to use, you don't even need to know how to use a spreadsheet though that can be a functional alternative.

MYTH: You Don't Need To Save (especially if you're not planning on making big money purchases)

While you may not be looking to invest your money, you can't possibly know what may happen 2,3 even 10 months into the future. You may think your job is secure, but what if the building burns down? What if you're in an accident and can't work? What if your spouse dies? There are so many "what if's" in the world that it's insane not to want to save money. Even if you're not looking to buy big purchases with your saved cash, being prepared can mean the difference in survival when the unexpected happens. Budgeting is a survival skill, you may not need it right now, but when bad things happen you'll be glad you have it.

Your Current Budget Isn't Working

About 80% of the population are in debt. You may have heard about the debt crisis, and felt the effects of the economic bubble bursting, but these words probably mean nothing to you as an average person. The problem with debt is that you're spending money that is not yours. Many of us use credit cards to make up the gap we have financially between the things we want and the things we can afford. We're living a lifestyle we can't actually afford and it's putting us into debt. We all have a budget, even if we fail to recognize it as such, a rough monetary amount that we stick within each month. If your income is $2700 a month, then you know full well that that $2000 designer dress is outside of your budget, or you should if you have any common sense.

One of the biggest reasons that your budget is failing is because your expenses are higher than your income. You're making less money than you're spending. The problem has nothing to do with your budgeting skills, it's your spending that is the issue. If you're a born spender than this can be the most difficult part of budgeting, and it may feel like punishment at first. Learning to live within your means is the first, and most important, hard rule of budgeting. If you plan to pay down your level of debt, then you'll either need to stick within that budget or even begin living below your means to generate a little more flexibility.

Another reason that your budget may be failing is that you're a spender that is struggling because you feel deprived of your fun. You're missing the rush of spending and the happiness it brings. While you should try and find other things that make you happy a budget that is too strict can be no budget at all as you may end up binging as if you were on a diet. A budget doesn't mean you can't have fun. It means you can have fun, but there's a limited amount of money allotted to it.

Probably the biggest "oops" of budgeters is that they still try and live "to their means". What this means, is that when these consumers get paid every week they allot every single penny into categories. They're not only not saving, but they're not factoring in expenses that might not occur every week (such as emergencies) and when they do they're going to feel a painful pinch. A great example of this is insurance premiums. Often paying your premium off in a lump sum can save you hundreds, but the convenience of being able to spread it out costs us dearly. If you could afford to pay off that lump sum when it was due wouldn't that be a better choice? Similarly, property taxes only come once a year, but you'll still need to budget them in or you'll find that month is extremely tight and you need to pull the money from somewhere else.

Budgeting is a Tool

Rather than seeing your budget as the financial end start seeing it as the road that gets you where you want to be. Many people find themselves getting bogged down in the facts and figures of their budget and it makes them unhappy by causing them stress. Rather than worrying that your budget isn't balanced or chasing every little penny if you're finding the experience stressful, try stepping back and simply ignoring the numbers but still trying to spend your money smarter.

Exercise: If you could save up the money what would you do with it? A good budget not only pays your bills, but also allows you to save up towards bigger and better goals. What sort of financial goals do you have? Would you like to pay off your debts? Would saving for a down payment on a house get you out of the rent cycle?

Now that you've identified a financial goal for yourself, you'll need a plan to get there. A budget is that tool. What your budget is going to do is pay your bills, allow you to put some money aside, and still feel like you're living your life. Once you've gotten the hang of how budgeting works you shouldn't even need the software anymore. A successful budget is one that doesn't drive you to distraction chasing every penny, but that you know is there and can check on from time to time. It sets out the ground rules for how you can play week for week.

Chapter 3 - Budgeting Basics

A successful budget is nothing more than a balance. It is the balance of income vs spending, nothing more. When it comes to actually creating a budget what you want to do is to know your habits, your spending, and your income. Your income and your spending are by far the most important, without an income you couldn't spend and if you didn't spend you wouldn't have the need for a budget.

Growing Income

How do you make money? If you get up every day and go to work, then you have an income. Maybe you're self-employed or own a business. The problem with being an employee is that it's not the road to success. No one who is successful works for someone else. Starting your own business can be a scary thought, and if you're not in a financial position to do so, then your only option for growing your income is going to be a promotion or a raise. Rather than counting on that raise you're going to need to look at alternative ways of making money. Do you have any skills? Is there anything someone else would pay you for (legally)?

Exercise: Think of ways you could make money. Do you have extra clothes in your closet that could go on eBay? Children's toys that are no longer wanted? Are you a closet writer or artist? Many of us have skills and items that could be used to make extra cash.

Successful people do not have one income. You may think that because both you and your spouse work that you have two incomes so this doesn't apply. But what if one of you lost their job or couldn't work? What would happen? This is why many people have a second business or side way of making extra cash.

For example, if you love shopping, perhaps you can turn that into a business. Personal shoppers are well paid, mystery shoppers are always in demand. Alternatively, if you have a lot of local thrift stores, could you buy items cheap there and resell them to make money? There are many ways to turn a negative habit into a way of making money.

By growing your income, and having more than one source, you'll not only have less of a pinch in your budget, but you'll also be able to stretch your money further because you'll have more.

Tracking Your Income

While you may not be looking to make extra money, you will still need to know exactly how much money you're bringing into your budget every month. So, how do you make money? A simple way of tracking your income would be an app, but if you've got bank statements that will work too.

Exercise: Take your bank statements for the month and on a piece of paper list all the money that goes into your account. Now think of all the other ways you make money. Do you sell stuff online, or have a skill that you sell part time (E.g. Handyman etc). List the amounts you make each month under that. For the purpose of this exercise if your income is flexible after your you can paycheque average it. Your monthly income is the sum total of these amounts.

Let's go back to that $2700. That represents your. It is the total that you and your spouse bring in as an employee for someone else. The wife, however, sells old clothes online and makes an extra $200 a month (average), the husband often pays the cheque does odd jobs for some of the neighbours ($300). That means their income is no longer $2700, it is, in fact, $3200. Suddenly their income is magically higher because they've only been counting the pay stubs. This is why it is so important to track your income AND your spending. You'll often find you're spending even more than you think you are once you start tracking all your money.

Tracking Expenses

Do you keep your receipts? The majority of us crumples them up, throw them away or let them languish in a bag. They're trash. Even in this day and age where we can look at our purchases on our statements instantaneously, receipts can have a purpose. Receipts are a paper record of what you have spent, and by keeping track of them, you'll often find you're feeling more accountable. That $3 you spent on a latte each day is now a weekly spending of about $21 on coffee.

Exercise: Go to your purse, pocket, or wherever you throw your receipts. Take a guess how much you have spent with those receipts. Take them out and add them up on a piece of paper. How far off was your guess? Did you learn anything about what you spend the most money on?

If you're not looking to simply have an app that you log expenses into constantly, then receipts are your only way of doing this. Keep an envelope or a bag and place every receipt in there at the end of the day. If you didn't get a receipt write your own and add it to the bag. You'll be able to take them out and list them by day, week, and month to see just where you're spending your money.

It's a good idea to see if you're using cash, check, or cards with these too, as sometimes people will spend more money using a card than cash without realizing because they can't physically feel the money changing hands. Here is an example of a tracking log that you can print out and use for this purpose. It will help you identify whether you needed to spend that money and exactly how your money is being spent. The surplus refers to your total income over whatever period you choose to monitor.

Use this template for a day, and then for a week. Compare the information that you've discovered. Just having to be accountable to this one spreadsheet may have made you think twice about making certain purchases. Keep credit card transactions that you need to pay off later on there as they will still count as a bill when they become due, but by counting them as an expense and as a bill you're also going to be counting them twice. Doing this is going to help you to see this as debt rather than as simply an expense because you're also going to be paying interest on that amount as an expense.

Chapter 4 - Budgeting Methods

You should now be intimately familiar with the total amount of money you make, and the total amount of money you spend. How do your figures look? Is there anything about both of these figures that you particularly notice?

Firstly, you should be able to identify approximately how much money you spend on needs each month. For example, rent, food, electric, gas, water, car insurance. How much does that leave you? What you're doing here is budgeting on a very simple scale. You're identifying your expenses and whether they are necessary while recognizing that you're working within a set amount. It's all very well to do that with money you're already spent, however, what you want to be able to do is plan ahead with your money.

The Envelope Method

This is the simplest method of budgeting, and it's surprisingly popular. The idea is that you have several envelopes. When you get paid you divide the money into envelopes based on how the money needs to be allotted. For example, one envelope for rent, one for water, one for, food, one for car insurance, gas, etc. The biggest pitfall here is forgetting something so try to determine all of your bills beforehand and also creating a blank envelope for savings and emergencies. Based on the information you learned last chapter if you were to cover all your needs, how would you divide up the money?

If you're working with the $3200 budget, then you're weekly allowance is $800. This might seem like a lot, but don't forget you have to take bills out of that money too. For the $3200 a month, $800 is rent, $200 is electric, $100 is car insurance, $200 for water, $200 credit card payment. These are your bills. These are papers that come through the mail and you can physically add up, they are fixed expenses. Add up your physical bills. In this instance the physical bills are $1500, that means that each week the family needs to put aside $375 to make sure the bills are covered in a 4 pay week month. (Ideally you should be paying more than the minimum balance on your credit cards to bring the amount down, once it starts to decrease continue paying the same amount and it will be paid off much quicker.) How much money is left?

The family has $1700 left for food, gas, and other expenses. This means they have $425 per week to spend on these things. These are variable expenses because this amount may fluctuate a little each week.

Look at your spreadsheet again. Roughly how much did you spend on those items? Did you spend more on food than gas? What were your other expenses that were not billed?

Each week the family gets $800, the total amount is taken in cash rather than left in the bank. $375 of that money is divided into the envelopes for bills. The remaining $425 needs to be split between the necessary expenses, savings and another envelope for wanting/fun.

At the end of the week if you have excess money in any of the necessities envelopes it can go towards the following week or be put aside for savings or wants.

Why It Works

If you have a habit of spending on credit cards or on any other cards and not being good at keeping track of how much you've spent then having cash can make you more mindful of how much you have to work with on any given day. It can also make you more accountable because you can physically see how much you're working with. By dividing your expenses week by week, you're not simply expecting your final pay cheque of the month to cover everything while being pinched for the other expenses that week. This is the simplest budgeting technique because you don't need any software, you simply need to have a rough grasp of where your money gets spent each week.

Budgeting By payday

Budgeting by payday works the same as the envelope method only you're not taking the money in cash. If you're doing this it's a good idea to have a separate account for fixed expense money to transfer to when you get paid, and you can also set up a direct transfer the day before your paycheque hits for any money left over from the week to go directly into a savings account. A lot of people don't like having multiple accounts to keep track of. This is why this method isn't necessarily as popular. In fact, it's the most common method for those who don't realize they are budgeting. Unless you're really spending a lot on your credit cards you're probably using some version of this method already.

Why It Works

For those that aren't necessarily spending excess money on cards because they're not physically aware of, it is a cash equivalent, this works perfectly. You'll also be able to see your bottom line of expenditures using just your bank account. Most bank accounts will show figures for money in/money out transactions which will negate the need to keep track using the software. By setting the money to be debited to a separate account and then direct paying your bills from that account for fixed expenses automatically you never have to forget to pay a bill. Not only that, but you'll only have the amount for variable expenses available to you at any given time so you won't be tempted or able to spend more and be short on your bills.

Budgeting by 50/20/30

The 50/20/30 method is simply a breakdown of expenses. If you're looking for a budgeting method that isn't as strict as the previous two this can work well. The idea is that you should have no more than 50% of your income dedicated to fixed costs (bills), 20% to an emergency fund or savings, and 30% for variable expenses. The percentages are meant to be a guideline rather than a strict budget so that you'll be more in control of your spending. If we go back to the same figures of the family budget a family that has a take home income of $3200 but bills of $1500 is actually well within this range since they're only spending 47%, of their remaining income they would then have $510 for flexible expenses and $340 for savings each month if they wanted to stick strictly to the 50/30/20 ratio. Not bad for a family with an income of $38,400 a year!

Why It Works

The reason this method works is mostly because of the 50 figure. Because the majority of living expenses is something that is not a flexible expense we *have* to pay that amount each month, but we still need enough to cover other expenses. By limited fixed bills to 50% you're working with a manageable figure. If you're calculating your fixed expenses at more than that then you're probably living beyond your means - maybe you don't need that luxury car, maybe you don't need the 5 bedroom house if you've only got 2 kids. This method is all about balance, it's about giving yourself room to live while still having manageable expenses. How do your finances measure up to this ratio?

Chapter 5 - How to Stretch Your Budget

Grocery Budgeting Tips

Groceries are usually the largest flexible expense you'll be dealing with. As a flexible expense, though it also means you have some room to work within it to make that budget go further. In fact, groceries are the number one place you can usually cut significantly to stretch your budget further.

- Look for sale or clearance items. Every week you get a flyer from your local grocery store, but how many times do you read it? If the specials aren't something you need this week are they something that can be frozen or prepared for next week? Similarly, many clearance items are still good, the packaging may be slightly damaged or they may be close to expiring, but if you're going to use them immediately that shouldn't be an issue. Always check this section out.

- Even if you're not up to the stage of extreme couponing yet coupons are still a great way to save money. Many stores accept competitors coupons too, so you're not going to be forced to shop around just to get the same deal. Register with manufacturers as well as stores for extra coupons. Some companies will also send you free samples if you ask for them.

- Try and set yourself a budget for food each day. There are many blogs that offer meal plans for $5 a day or less. If you're calculating for leftovers this can mean an even lower cost per meal.

- Plan ahead rather than just wandering the aisles. A lot of the time we end up buying things we don't need or taking multiple trips because we didn't plan our meals for the week. Just as being able to budget a certain amount of food each day works well planning the meals will help you stick to that budget.

⅄ Many people will tell you that generic isn't the same as brand name items, but often these items are produced in the same factory by the same company just with a different packaging. They're far cheaper and will save you a lot of money over the long term. This applies to prescriptions and medications as well.

⅄ If you use a lot of any one item consider buying it from a bulk store. Often bulk items like beans, frozen vegetables, or snacks are far cheaper in these places than simply purchasing them from the regular grocery store.

⅄ Go Meatless. Meat is often the most expensive item on a grocery list. Even choosing to go meatless one night a week and swapping for alternative protein like beans or soy can save you a significant amount of money. It's also good for the planet.

Other Ways to Save

⅄ Sign up for programs that you're eligible for. For example, if you have children social services may be able to help you get a lower rate on your utilities. There are many different private and government programs that can help with your utility bills. If you're not already using these look into them and see what you're eligible for.

⅄ Do you really need the latest phone and all that data? Most places have wifi these days, so unless you're driving long distances or don't have home internet consider lowering your data package. Most companies will let you look over your usage to see what you're working with. Rather than paying overages consider swapping from one of the main carriers to a smaller pay as you go company. Many of the PAYG companies have far lower rates and will let you bring your own phone and number. Potentially you could cut your phone bill in half.

⋏ Do you have a cable subscription as well as the internet? Most television shows are available to watch online, and you can also pay for subscription services through the internet at a fraction of the cost of your cable bill. Unless you're dead set on your satellite or cable company you can actually remove this bill altogether by watching your shows online.

⋏ Curb your takeout habit. Some families eat out up to 5 nights a week. This is hugely expensive and unnecessary. Treating yourself every now and then is fine, or on a night when you know you're going to be too tired but consider cooking at home. The same dishes will be cheaper and healthier. If you really can't face the thought of cooking look at slow cooker recipes that can be left to cook all day while you're at work and ready when you walk in the door.

⋏ Look for free activities you can get involved in. Rather than paying for bowling or movies each week have a look at other local events that are going on. Many towns have an events calendar with galleries, film, art, and other activities that are all free. Not only will you save money, but you'll also be doing a cultural or educational activity for the whole family.

⋏ If you have one nix your gym membership. Gym memberships are fun, but entirely unnecessary. You can walk or run for free in your own neighbourhood or at the local park. Look at yard sales or online for used weights and machines and you'll spend far less than you do annually on a gym membership.

Frugal Living

One of the trends among Millennials is living with less. Frugal living is an ideal way to stretch out your budget. Simply put, it's choosing to live below your means so that you're in a better place financially. Frugal living isn't all about recycling and giving up everything you enjoy. It's about making a smarter choice to spend less than you could be. Living frugally is often a good way of lowering your fixed expenses, something that you may not have thought possible.

- Buy Second hand or go to swap-meets. Many kids items can be found almost new or even new at thrift stores, online and at local swap meets. Rather than shelling out at the mall, consider finding clothes and toys cheaper elsewhere.

- Do you really need two cars? Most familiar have multiple vehicles because it's to be expected, but do you need them? If you can take public transport or ride-share you'll not only cut out a car payment, you'll lower your insurance and your gas costs phenomenally. The car is probably second on your list of fixed expenses by cost, so if you can lower that amount do it. Similarly, if you don't need that big, luxury vehicle, consider trading it in for a smaller used car and a lower payment instead.

- Conserving your utilities might sound difficult, but often we're very guilty of wasting our electric and water bills. For example, did you know that by leaving electronics plugged in they're still using power? That little light that shows the device is still plugged into costs electricity. Similarly, walking out of a room and leaving the light on is the biggest drain on your power bill. Make a habit to switch off and unplug items you're not using. If you haven't already swapped to energy saving bulbs do so, and consider wrapping your windows in clear plastic to help insulate better.

- Buy a clothes line. If you've got a garden you can cut out the electricity needed to run your dryer by simply hanging clothes out the same way your parents did. You'd be amazed at how much this can lower your electric bill.

- ⚑ DIY. Many of those simple household chores can be done yourself. Instead of hiring a handyman, consider looking on YouTube for instructions. Obviously, if you're looking at rewiring the house, it's safer to call a professional, but if you just need the gutters cleaned or the sink unblocked you're probably going to save a lot of money doing it yourself.

- ⚑ Reduce your interest. No matter how much debt you have, you're paying a significant portion of your monthly bills in interest. If you've been paying on your car or house for a while consider having them refinanced and cutting your rate, not only will you lower your monthly bill but you may also have a better rate than before. If you do manage to lower the bill consider continuing to pay the same amount as before as this will lower your debt and help you pay the item off quickly.

Conclusion

Budgeting doesn't have to be boring, and it's certainly not hard. A good budget is all about being able to live with your money while still being smart about how you use it.

No matter which budgeting method appeals to you, you can do this.

Start your budgeting today by calculating your income, expenses, and seeing where you can stretch that amount. Could you possibly make more money on the side? Could you possibly spend less at the grocery store?

Once you know the ins and outs of your financial choices you can make those choices better ones.

Hopefully, you've learned a lot about how to gauge your financial health and how to improve it.

Thank you for downloading this book, please take the time to share your thoughts and post a review on Amazon. It will be greatly appreciated!

-- Author

www.ingramcontent.com/pod-product-compliance
Lightning Source LLC
Chambersburg PA
CBHW070308190526
45169CB00004B/1548